ONE LIST A DAY

A THREE-YEAR JOURNAL

CREATED BY

LISA NOLA

ILLUSTRATIONS BY

HARRIET TAYLOR SEED

CHRONICLE BOOKS

SAN FRANCISCO

ISBN 978-1-4521-6444-1

Manufactured in China

MIX
Paper from
responsible sources
FSC™ C136333

Design by Lizzie Vaughan
Illustrations by Harriet Taylor Seed

**See the full range of Listography
products at www.chroniclebooks.com**

Chronicle Books publishes distinctive books and gifts. From
award-winning children's titles, bestselling cookbooks, and eclectic
pop culture to acclaimed works of art and design, stationery, and
journals, we craft publishing that's instantly recognizable for its
spirit and creativity. Enjoy our publishing and become part of our
community at www.chroniclebooks.com.

1 0 9 8 7

Chronicle Books LLC.
680 Second Street
San Francisco, California 94107

www.chroniclebooks.com

INTRODUCTION

LISTS ARE A FUN AND EASY WAY TO CAPTURE YOUR STORY. FEATURING A DIFFERENT LIST TOPIC EVERY DAY, THIS JOURNAL ENCOURAGES YOU TO TAP INTO YOUR CREATIVITY AND EXPAND YOUR IMAGINATION.

START WHENEVER YOU LIKE—SIMPLY OPEN TO TODAY'S DATE, FILL IN THE YEAR, AND MAKE A LITTLE LIST. SOME OF THESE TOPICS WILL BRING BACK MEMORIES, OTHERS WILL ASK YOU TO THINK ABOUT THE PRESENT MOMENT OR THE FUTURE. EACH MONTH BEGINS WITH A LITTLE TO-DO LIST AND ENDS WITH A HAPPINESS LIST. AFTER THREE YEARS, AS YOU REVISIT AND EXPAND YOUR LISTS, YOU'LL FIND THAT YOU HAVE CREATED A UNIQUE TIME CAPSULE AND A MINI-AUTOBIOGRAPHY.

HAVE FUN!

LISA NOLA
WWW.LISTOGRAPHY.COM

TOP GOALS FOR THIS YEAR

20 ___

- _____
- _____
- _____

20 ___

- _____
- _____
- _____

20 ___

- _____
- _____
- _____

WORDS THAT CAPTURE
WHO I AM

20 _____

- _____
- _____
- _____

20 _____

- _____
- _____
- _____

20 _____

- _____
- _____
- _____

HOW MY LIFE IS DIFFERENT
FROM LAST YEAR

20 _____

- _____
- _____
- _____

20 _____

- _____
- _____
- _____

20 _____

- _____
- _____
- _____

ADVICE TO MYSELF
FOR THE COMING YEAR

20 _____

- _____
- _____
- _____

20 _____

- _____
- _____
- _____

20 _____

- _____
- _____
- _____

PLACES I WANT
TO GO THIS YEAR

20 _____

- _____

- _____

- _____

20 _____

- _____

- _____

- _____

20 _____

- _____

- _____

- _____

VALUES TO FOCUS
ON THIS YEAR

20 _____

- _____
- _____
- _____

20 _____

- _____
- _____
- _____

20 _____

- _____
- _____
- _____

THINGS TO STAY AWAY
FROM THIS YEAR

20 _____

- _____

- _____

- _____

20 _____

- _____

- _____

- _____

20 _____

- _____

- _____

- _____

PEOPLE WHO HAVE
INFLUENCED ME

20 _____

- _____
- _____
- _____

20 _____

- _____
- _____
- _____

20 _____

- _____
- _____
- _____

LITTLE THINGS I APPRECIATE

20 _____

- _____
- _____
- _____

20 _____

- _____
- _____
- _____

20 _____

- _____
- _____
- _____

NEW RESTAURANTS TO TRY

20 ____

- _____
- _____
- _____

20 ____

- _____
- _____
- _____

20 ____

- _____
- _____
- _____

I'D LOVE TO BE A FLY ON THE WALL IN THESE ROOMS

20 _____

- _____
- _____
- _____

20 _____

- _____
- _____
- _____

20 _____

- _____
- _____
- _____

THINGS THAT GOT ON MY NERVES RECENTLY

20 _____

- _____
- _____
- _____

20 _____

- _____
- _____
- _____

20 _____

- _____
- _____
- _____

IF I COULD HAVE ANY TALENT OR SKILL, IT WOULD BE...

20 _____

- _____
- _____
- _____

20 _____

- _____
- _____
- _____

20 _____

- _____
- _____
- _____

EVENTS THAT
CHANGED ME

20 ___

- --
- --
- --

20 ___

- --
- --
- --

20 ___

- --
- --
- --

THINGS TO DO
ON MY DAY OFF

20 ___

- _____
- _____
- _____

20 ___

- _____
- _____
- _____

20 ___

- _____
- _____
- _____

TV SHOWS TO WATCH

20 _____

- _____
- _____
- _____

20 _____

- _____
- _____
- _____

20 _____

- _____
- _____
- _____

A FEW THINGS ABOUT
MY PARENT(S)

20 _____

- _____
- _____
- _____

20 _____

- _____
- _____
- _____

20 _____

- _____
- _____
- _____

MY PHOBIAS

20 ____

- ------------------------------
- ------------------------------
- ------------------------------

20 ____

- ------------------------------
- ------------------------------
- ------------------------------

20 ____

- ------------------------------
- ------------------------------
- ------------------------------

SOME ACHIEVEMENTS
I'VE MADE SO FAR

20 _____

- _____
- _____
- _____

20 _____

- _____
- _____
- _____

20 _____

- _____
- _____
- _____

CURRENT FOOD
OBSESSIONS

20 _____

- _____
- _____
- _____

20 _____

- _____
- _____
- _____

20 _____

- _____
- _____
- _____

CURRENT STRESSES

20 _____

- _____
- _____
- _____

20 _____

- _____
- _____
- _____

20 _____

- _____
- _____
- _____

NICE THINGS I'D SAY
ABOUT MYSELF TODAY

20 _____

- _____
- _____
- _____

20 _____

- _____
- _____
- _____

20 _____

- _____
- _____
- _____

INTERESTING NEWS STORIES
RIGHT NOW

20 _____

- _____
- _____
- _____

20 _____

- _____
- _____
- _____

20 _____

- _____
- _____
- _____

IF I WERE AN ANIMAL,
I'D BE...

20 _____

- _____
- _____
- _____

20 _____

- _____
- _____
- _____

20 _____

- _____
- _____
- _____

THINGS TO SAVE UP FOR

20 ____

- _____
- _____
- _____

20 ____

- _____
- _____
- _____

20 ____

- _____
- _____
- _____

THREE PEOPLE I
COULDN'T LIVE WITHOUT

20 ____

- _____
- _____
- _____

20 ____

- _____
- _____
- _____

20 ____

- _____
- _____
- _____

BOOKS THAT
INFLUENCED ME

20 ____

- _____
- _____
- _____

20 ____

- _____
- _____
- _____

20 ____

- _____
- _____
- _____

DREAM JOBS

20 _____
- _____
- _____
- _____

20 _____
- _____
- _____
- _____

20 _____
- _____
- _____
- _____

RECENT INSPIRATIONS

20 _____

- _____
- _____
- _____

20 _____

- _____
- _____
- _____

20 _____

- _____
- _____
- _____

SOME THINGS I DID
THIS WEEK

20 _____

- _____
- _____
- _____

20 _____

- _____
- _____
- _____

20 _____

- _____
- _____
- _____

THINGS THAT MADE ME
HAPPY THIS MONTH

20 _____

- _____
- _____
- _____

20 _____

- _____
- _____
- _____

20 _____

- _____
- _____
- _____

THIS MONTH'S LITTLE
TO-DO LIST

20 _____

- _____

- _____

- _____

20 _____

- _____

- _____

- _____

20 _____

- _____

- _____

- _____

DATE IDEAS

20 ___

- _____
- _____
- _____

20 ___

- _____
- _____
- _____

20 ___

- _____
- _____
- _____

THREE SECRETS ABOUT ME

20 _____

- _____
- _____
- _____

20 _____

- _____
- _____
- _____

20 _____

- _____
- _____
- _____

CONCERTS
I'D TIME TRAVEL TO

20 _____

- _____
- _____
- _____

20 _____

- _____
- _____
- _____

20 _____

- _____
- _____
- _____

HOW TO WIN MY HEART

20 _____

- _____
- _____
- _____

20 _____

- _____
- _____
- _____

20 _____

- _____
- _____
- _____

THINGS I LOVE ABOUT
THE '90S ERA

20 _____

- _____
- _____
- _____

20 _____

- _____
- _____
- _____

20 _____

- _____
- _____
- _____

WEBSITES I LOVE

20 _____

- _____
- _____
- _____

20 _____

- _____
- _____
- _____

20 _____

- _____
- _____
- _____

SOME STUFF I'M GREAT AT

20 _____

- _____
- _____
- _____

20 _____

- _____
- _____
- _____

20 _____

- _____
- _____
- _____

THINGS THAT
MAKE ME LAUGH

20 ___

- _____
- _____
- _____

20 ___

- _____
- _____
- _____

20 ___

- _____
- _____
- _____

WEIRD THINGS I DO

20 ___

- _____
- _____
- _____

20 ___

-) _____
- _____
- _____

20 ___

- _____
- _____
- _____

WHAT I'D HAVE ON MY FARM

20 ____

- _____
- _____
- _____

20 ____

- _____
- _____
- _____

20 ____

- _____
- _____
- _____

SONGS THAT CAPTURE ME

20 _____

- _____
- _____
- _____

20 _____

- _____
- _____
- _____

20 _____

- _____
- _____
- _____

IDEAS FOR LOCAL
WEEKEND GETAWAYS

20 _____

- _____
- _____
- _____

20 _____

- _____
- _____
- _____

20 _____

- _____
- _____
- _____

I LOVE...

20 ___

- --
- --
- --

20 ___

- --
- --
- --

20 ___

- --
- --
- --

THINGS I WANT
TO LEARN TO COOK

20 _____

- _____
- _____
- _____

20 _____

- _____
- _____
- _____

20 _____

- _____
- _____
- _____

CURRENT COMPLAINTS

20 _____

- _____
- _____
- _____

20 _____

- _____
- _____
- _____

20 _____

- _____
- _____
- _____

CURRENT MALE CRUSHES

20 _____

- _____
- _____
- _____

20 _____

- _____
- _____
- _____

20 _____

- _____
- _____
- _____

WHAT I HOPE TO ACCOMPLISH IN MY LIFETIME

20 _____

- _____
- _____
- _____

20 _____

- _____
- _____
- _____

20 _____

- _____
- _____
- _____

WISDOM I'D GIVE TO MY YOUNGER SELF

20 ____

- ----------------------------------
- ----------------------------------
- ----------------------------------

20 ____

- ----------------------------------
- ----------------------------------
- ----------------------------------

20 ____

- ----------------------------------
- ----------------------------------
- ----------------------------------

CAUSES I'D LOVE TO
VOLUNTEER FOR

20 ____

- _____
- _____
- _____

20 ____

- _____
- _____
- _____

20 ____

- _____
- _____
- _____

SOME CHILDHOOD MEMORIES

20 _____

- _____
- _____
- _____

20 _____

- _____
- _____
- _____

20 _____

- _____
- _____
- _____

FADS AND TRENDS
I'VE TAKEN PART IN

20 ____

- _____
- _____
- _____

20 ____

- _____
- _____
- _____

20 ____

- _____
- _____
- _____

I HOPE I WAS _____ IN MY FORMER LIFE

20 ____

- _____
- _____
- _____

20 ____

- _____
- _____
- _____

20 ____

- _____
- _____
- _____

RECENT TRANSGRESSIONS

20 _____

- _____
- _____
- _____

20 _____

- _____
- _____
- _____

20 _____

- _____
- _____
- _____

RANDOM THOUGHTS TODAY

20 _____

- ------------------------------
- ------------------------------
- ------------------------------

20 _____

- ------------------------------
- ------------------------------
- ------------------------------

20 _____

- ------------------------------
- ------------------------------
- ------------------------------

LISTS I SHOULD MAKE

20 _____

- _____
- _____
- _____

20 _____

- _____
- _____
- _____

20 _____

- _____
- _____
- _____

FAVORITE GIFTS TO RECEIVE

20 _____

- _____
- _____
- _____

20 _____

- _____
- _____
- _____

20 _____

- _____
- _____
- _____

THINGS THAT MAKE ME CRY

20 _____

- _____
- _____
- _____

20 _____

- _____
- _____
- _____

20 _____

- _____
- _____
- _____

THINGS THAT MADE ME
HAPPY THIS MONTH

20 _____

- _____
- _____
- _____

20 _____

- _____
- _____
- _____

20 _____

- _____
- _____
- _____

THIS MONTH'S LITTLE TO-DO LIST

20 _____

- _____
- _____
- _____

20 _____

- _____
- _____
- _____

20 _____

- _____
- _____
- _____

IDEAS FOR
GETTING HEALTHY

20 ____

- _____
- _____
- _____

20 ____

- _____
- _____
- _____

20 ____

- _____
- _____
- _____

A FEW RANDOM MEMORIES

20 _____

- _____
- _____
- _____

20 _____

- _____
- _____
- _____

20 _____

- _____
- _____
- _____

CURRENT FAVORITE ACTORS AND ACTRESSES

20 ____

- _____
- _____
- _____

20 ____

- _____
- _____
- _____

20 ____

- _____
- _____
- _____

STUFF I'VE GOOGLED RECENTLY

20 _____

- _____
- _____
- _____

20 _____

- _____
- _____
- _____

20 _____

- _____
- _____
- _____

PETS I'VE HAD OR WOULD LIKE TO HAVE

20 _____

- _____
- _____
- _____

20 _____

- _____
- _____
- _____

20 _____

- _____
- _____
- _____

IF I LOST THE ABILITY TO TASTE, I'D MISS TASTING...

20 ___

- _____
- _____
- _____

20 ___

- _____
- _____
- _____

20 ___

- _____
- _____
- _____

THINGS I GOT IN TROUBLE FOR AS A KID

20 ___

- _____
- _____
- _____

20 ___

- _____
- _____
- _____

20 ___

- _____
- _____
- _____

SOME STUFF I'M JUST NOT GOOD AT

20 _____

- _____
- _____
- _____

20 _____

- _____
- _____
- _____

20 _____

- _____
- _____
- _____

CLASSES I'D LOVE TO TAKE

20 _____

- _____
- _____
- _____

20 _____

- _____
- _____
- _____

20 _____

- _____
- _____
- _____

STORIES MY FAMILY MEMBERS OFTEN SHARE

20 _____

- _____
- _____
- _____

20 _____

- _____
- _____
- _____

20 _____

- _____
- _____
- _____

CURRENT DAYDREAMS

20 _____

- _____
- _____
- _____

20 _____

- _____
- _____
- _____

20 _____

- _____
- _____
- _____

MEMORABLE WORK MOMENTS

20 _____

- _____
- _____
- _____

20 _____

- _____
- _____
- _____

20 _____

- _____
- _____
- _____

REASONS FOR MY
RECENT GOOD MOODS

20 _____

- _____
- _____
- _____

20 _____

- _____
- _____
- _____

20 _____

- _____
- _____
- _____

PET PEEVES

20 _____

- _____
- _____
- _____

20 _____

- _____
- _____
- _____

20 _____

- _____
- _____
- _____

I'D LIKE TO PUT
MORE ENERGY INTO...

20 _____

- _____
- _____
- _____

20 _____

- _____
- _____
- _____

20 _____

- _____
- _____
- _____

SOCIAL CHANGE
I WANT TO SEE

20 _____

- _____
- _____
- _____

20 _____

- _____
- _____
- _____

20 _____

- _____
- _____
- _____

WORDS TO DESCRIBE
MYSELF TODAY

20 _____

- _____
- _____
- _____

20 _____

- _____
- _____
- _____

20 _____

- _____
- _____
- _____

LAST THREE
MOVIES WATCHED

20 _____

- - - - - - - - - - - - - - - - - -

- - - - - - - - - - - - - - - - - -

- - - - - - - - - - - - - - - - - -

20 _____

- - - - - - - - - - - - - - - - - -

- - - - - - - - - - - - - - - - - -

- - - - - - - - - - - - - - - - - -

20 _____

- - - - - - - - - - - - - - - - - -

- - - - - - - - - - - - - - - - - -

- - - - - - - - - - - - - - - - - -

SOUNDS I DISLIKE

20 ____

- _____
- _____
- _____

20 ____

- _____
- _____
- _____

20 ____

- _____
- _____
- _____

WISHES FOR MY FUTURE

20 _____

- _____
- _____
- _____

20 _____

- _____
- _____
- _____

20 _____

- _____
- _____
- _____

CURRENT FAVORITE SHOPS

20 _____

- _____
- _____
- _____

20 _____

- _____
- _____
- _____

20 _____

- _____
- _____
- _____

THINGS THAT MADE
ME SAD RECENTLY

20 _____

- _____
- _____
- _____

20 _____

- _____
- _____
- _____

20 _____

- _____
- _____
- _____

I'M SO LUCKY BECAUSE...

20 _____

- _____
- _____
- _____

20 _____

- _____
- _____
- _____

20 _____

- _____
- _____
- _____

MEMORABLE THINGS
I'VE TOUCHED

20 ___

- _____
- _____
- _____

20 ___

- _____
- _____
- _____

20 ___

- _____
- _____
- _____

MY PASSIONS

20 _____

- _____
- _____
- _____

20 _____

- _____
- _____
- _____

20 _____

- _____
- _____
- _____

IDENTIFIABLE FEATURES ON MY BODY

20 ____

- _____
- _____
- _____

20 ____

- _____
- _____
- _____

20 ____

- _____
- _____
- _____

IF I WERE TO CHANGE MY NAME, IT WOULD BE...

20 _____

- _____
- _____
- _____

20 _____

- _____
- _____
- _____

20 _____

- _____
- _____
- _____

I'M GUILTY OF...

20 _____

- _____
- _____
- _____

20 _____

- _____
- _____
- _____

20 _____

- _____
- _____
- _____

RECENT CHALLENGES

20 _____

- _____
- _____
- _____

20 _____

- _____
- _____
- _____

20 _____

- _____
- _____
- _____

THINGS THAT MADE ME
HAPPY THIS MONTH

20 ___

- ------------------------------
- ------------------------------
- ------------------------------

20 ___

- ------------------------------
- ------------------------------
- ------------------------------

20 ___

- ------------------------------
- ------------------------------
- ------------------------------

THIS MONTH'S LITTLE
TO-DO LIST

20 _____

- _____

- _____

- _____

20 _____

- _____

- _____

- _____

20 _____

- _____

- _____

- _____

UNIQUE PLACES I'VE VISITED

20 _____

- _____
- _____
- _____

20 _____

- _____
- _____
- _____

20 _____

- _____
- _____
- _____

SOME EMBARRASSING
MOMENTS

20 _____

- _____
- _____
- _____

20 _____

- _____
- _____
- _____

20 _____

- _____
- _____
- _____

FOODS I WANT TO TRY

20 _____

- _____
- _____
- _____

20 _____

- _____
- _____
- _____

20 _____

- _____
- _____
- _____

MOVIE SCENES I WOULD HAVE LOVED TO BE AN EXTRA IN

20 ___

- _____
- _____
- _____

20 ___

- _____
- _____
- _____

20 ___

- _____
- _____
- _____

THINGS TO CHECK OUT
IN MY CITY

20 _____

- _____
- _____
- _____

20 _____

- _____
- _____
- _____

20 _____

- _____
- _____
- _____

WHAT I LOVE
ABOUT _____

20 _____

- _____
- _____
- _____

20 _____

- _____
- _____
- _____

20 _____

- _____
- _____
- _____

A FEW THINGS
I'VE NOTICED RECENTLY

20 ___

- _____
- _____
- _____

20 ___

- _____
- _____
- _____

20 ___

- _____
- _____
- _____

I WISH I KNEW
WHAT IT FELT LIKE TO...

20 _____

- _____
- _____
- _____

20 _____

- _____
- _____
- _____

20 _____

- _____
- _____
- _____

HOME IMPROVEMENT IDEAS

20 _____

- _____
- _____
- _____

20 _____

- _____
- _____
- _____

20 _____

- _____
- _____
- _____

MEMORABLE SOUNDS
FROM MY LIFE

20 _____

- _____
- _____
- _____

20 _____

- _____
- _____
- _____

20 _____

- _____
- _____
- _____

IF I HAD NINE LIVES,
I WOULD...

20 _____

- _____
- _____
- _____

20 _____

- _____
- _____
- _____

20 _____

- _____
- _____
- _____

TIMES I'VE BEEN
THE MOST SURPRISED

20 ___

- _____
- _____
- _____

20 ___

- _____
- _____
- _____

20 ___

- _____
- _____
- _____

SONGS THAT DESCRIBE
MY MOOD TODAY

20 _____

- _____
- _____
- _____

20 _____

- _____
- _____
- _____

20 _____

- _____
- _____
- _____

SOME THINGS
I DID THIS WEEK

20 _____

- _____
- _____
- _____

20 _____

- _____
- _____
- _____

20 _____

- _____
- _____
- _____

A FEW THINGS
I'D CHANGE RIGHT NOW

20 _____

- _____
- _____
- _____

20 _____

- _____
- _____
- _____

20 _____

- _____
- _____
- _____

QUESTIONS FOR
THE UNIVERSE

20 _____

- _____
- _____
- _____

20 _____

- _____
- _____
- _____

20 _____

- _____
- _____
- _____

THINGS I MISS
THAT NO LONGER EXIST

20 _____

- _____
- _____
- _____

20 _____

- _____
- _____
- _____

20 _____

- _____
- _____
- _____

IF I COULD HAVE DINNER WITH ANYONE, IT WOULD BE...

20 ___

- _____
- _____
- _____

20 ___

- _____
- _____
- _____

20 ___

- _____
- _____
- _____

A PERFECT SUNDAY
WOULD INCLUDE...

20 _____

- _____
- _____
- _____

20 _____

- _____
- _____
- _____

20 _____

- _____
- _____
- _____

GOOD DEEDS I'VE DONE

20 ___

- _____
- _____
- _____

20 ___

- _____
- _____
- _____

20 ___

- _____
- _____
- _____

THINGS I'D RECOMMEND
TO OTHERS RIGHT NOW

20 _____

- _____
- _____
- _____

20 _____

- _____
- _____
- _____

20 _____

- _____
- _____
- _____

QUALITIES TO WORK
ON IN MYSELF

20 _____

- _____
- _____
- _____

20 _____

- _____
- _____
- _____

20 _____

- _____
- _____
- _____

APRIL 24

I DISLIKE...

20 _____

- _____
- _____
- _____

20 _____

- _____
- _____
- _____

20 _____

- _____
- _____
- _____

MY DREAM MUSIC
FESTIVAL LINE-UP

20 _____

- _____
- _____
- _____

20 _____

- _____
- _____
- _____

20 _____

- _____
- _____
- _____

THINGS I'M PROUD OF

20 _____

* _____
* _____
* _____

20 _____

* _____
* _____
* _____

20 _____

* _____
* _____
* _____

REASONS FOR MY
RECENT BAD MOODS

20 _____

- _____
- _____
- _____

20 _____

- _____
- _____
- _____

20 _____

- _____
- _____
- _____

MEMORABLE INJURIES

20 _____

- _____
- _____
- _____

20 _____

- _____
- _____
- _____

20 _____

- _____
- _____
- _____

FAVORITE WRITERS

20 _____

- _____
- _____
- _____

20 _____

- _____
- _____
- _____

20 _____

- _____
- _____
- _____

APRIL 30

THINGS THAT MADE ME HAPPY THIS MONTH

20 ___

- _____
- _____
- _____

20 ___

- _____
- _____
- _____

20 ___

- _____
- _____
- _____

CREATE YOUR OWN LIST

20 _____

- _____
- _____
- _____

20 _____

- _____
- _____
- _____

20 _____

- _____
- _____
- _____

THIS MONTH'S LITTLE
TO-DO LIST

20 ____

- _____
- _____
- _____

20 ____

- _____
- _____
- _____

20 ____

- _____
- _____
- _____

FILMS I CAN WATCH OVER AND OVER AGAIN

20 _____

- _____
- _____
- _____

20 _____

- _____
- _____
- _____

20 _____

- _____
- _____
- _____

THINGS THAT WERE AMAZING THE FIRST TIME I DID THEM

20 ___

- ___
- ___
- ___

20 ___

- ___
- ___
- ___

20 ___

- ___
- ___
- ___

WORDS I DISLIKE

20 _____

- _____
- _____
- _____

20 _____

- _____
- _____
- _____

20 _____

- _____
- _____
- _____

RECENT DISAPPOINTMENTS

20 _____

- _____
- _____
- _____

20 _____

- _____
- _____
- _____

20 _____

- _____
- _____
- _____

BEST LIVE PERFORMANCES
I'VE SEEN

20 _____

- _____

- _____

- _____

20 _____

- _____

- _____

- _____

20 _____

- _____

- _____

- _____

TOP NEWS STORIES
RIGHT NOW

20 _____

- _____
- _____
- _____

20 _____

- _____
- _____
- _____

20 _____

- _____
- _____
- _____

CREATIVE THINGS
I'D LIKE TO TRY

20 _____

- _____
- _____
- _____

20 _____

- _____
- _____
- _____

20 _____

- _____
- _____
- _____

RALLIES, MARCHES, OR PARADES I'VE BEEN TO

20 _____

- _____
- _____
- _____

20 _____

- _____
- _____
- _____

20 _____

- _____
- _____
- _____

SCHOOL-DAY CRUSHES

20 ___
- _____
- _____
- _____

20 ___
- _____
- _____
- _____

20 ___
- _____
- _____
- _____

MOST RECENT GET-TOGETHERS
WITH FRIENDS

20 ____

- _____
- _____
- _____

20 ____

- _____
- _____
- _____

20 ____

- _____
- _____
- _____

THINGS I CAN'T LIVE
WITHOUT RIGHT NOW

20 _____

- _____
- _____
- _____

20 _____

- _____
- _____
- _____

20 _____

- _____
- _____
- _____

EPITAPHS FOR MY TOMBSTONE

20 ___

- _____
- _____
- _____

20 ___

- _____
- _____
- _____

20 ___

- _____
- _____
- _____

MEMORIES WITH A PARENT

20 _____

- _____
- _____
- _____

20 _____

- _____
- _____
- _____

20 _____

- _____
- _____
- _____

WISHES FOR MY
COUNTRY'S FUTURE

20 ____

- _____
- _____
- _____

20 ____

- _____
- _____
- _____

20 ____

- _____
- _____
- _____

BIGGEST FEARS

20 ____

- ----
- ----
- ----

20 ____

- ----
- ----
- ----

20 ____

- ----
- ----
- ----

THINGS I LOVE
ABOUT THE '80S ERA

20 _____

- _____
- _____
- _____

20 _____

- _____
- _____
- _____

20 _____

- _____
- _____
- _____

MEMORABLE THINGS I'VE DONE FOR MY BIRTHDAY

20 _____

- _____
- _____
- _____

20 _____

- _____
- _____
- _____

20 _____

- _____
- _____
- _____

WORDS TO DESCRIBE
THE WORLD TODAY

20 _____

- _____
- _____
- _____

20 _____

- _____
- _____
- _____

20 _____

- _____
- _____
- _____

SOME MEMORABLE
COWORKERS FROM MY PAST

20 ___

- _____
- _____
- _____

20 ___

- _____
- _____
- _____

20 ___

- _____
- _____
- _____

FAVORITE SNACKS

20 _____

- _____
- _____
- _____

20 _____

- _____
- _____
- _____

20 _____

- _____
- _____
- _____

RANDOM THOUGHTS TODAY

20 _____

- ------------------------
- ------------------------
- ------------------------

20 _____

- ------------------------
- ------------------------
- ------------------------

20 _____

- ------------------------
- ------------------------
- ------------------------

THINGS I'VE LOST

20 _____

- _____
- _____
- _____

20 _____

- _____
- _____
- _____

20 _____

- _____
- _____
- _____

RULES TO LIVE BY

20 _____

- _____
- _____
- _____

20 _____

- _____
- _____
- _____

20 _____

- _____
- _____
- _____

HOW I'D SPEND
MY LAST DAY ON EARTH

20 ____

- _____
- _____
- _____

20 ____

- _____
- _____
- _____

20 ____

- _____
- _____
- _____

CURRENT HABITS OR
ROUTINES TO BREAK

20 ____

- _____
- _____
- _____

20 ____

- _____
- _____
- _____

20 ____

- _____
- _____
- _____

INTERNET GUILTY PLEASURES

20 _____

- _____
- _____
- _____

20 _____

- _____
- _____
- _____

20 _____

- _____
- _____
- _____

SUBJECTS I'D LIKE
TO KNOW MORE ABOUT

20 _____

- _____
- _____
- _____

20 _____

- _____
- _____
- _____

20 _____

- _____
- _____
- _____

TYPES OF ART I'D LOVE TO BE ABLE TO MAKE

20 ___

- _____
- _____
- _____

20 ___

- _____
- _____
- _____

20 ___

- _____
- _____
- _____

THINGS TO SEE
IN MY COUNTRY

20 _____

- _____
- _____
- _____

20 _____

- _____
- _____
- _____

20 _____

- _____
- _____
- _____

THINGS THAT MADE ME
HAPPY THIS MONTH

20 _____

- _____
- _____
- _____

20 _____

- _____
- _____
- _____

20 _____

- _____
- _____
- _____

THIS MONTH'S LITTLE TO-DO LIST

20 ____

- _____
- _____
- _____

20 ____

- _____
- _____
- _____

20 ____

- _____
- _____
- _____

BOOKS I'D LIKE TO READ

20 ____

- _____
- _____
- _____

20 ____

- _____
- _____
- _____

20 ____

- _____
- _____
- _____

GURUS OR TEACHERS
WHO INSPIRED ME

20 ____

- _____
- _____
- _____

20 ____

- _____
- _____
- _____

20 ____

- _____
- _____
- _____

SOUNDS I HEAR IN MY
DAY-TO-DAY THAT I LOVE

20 _____

- _____
- _____
- _____

20 _____

- _____
- _____
- _____

20 _____

- _____
- _____
- _____

FOOD-RELATED MEMORIES

20 ____

- _____
- _____
- _____

20 ____

- _____
- _____
- _____

20 ____

- _____
- _____
- _____

GOOD HABITS I'D
LOVE TO CREATE

20 _____

- _____
- _____
- _____

20 _____

- _____
- _____
- _____

20 _____

- _____
- _____
- _____

MEMORABLE DISAGREEMENTS
I'VE HAD WITH PEOPLE

20 _____

- _____
- _____
- _____

20 _____

- _____
- _____
- _____

20 _____

- _____
- _____
- _____

HOW I'D SPEND
LOTTERY WINNINGS

20 _____

- _____
- _____
- _____

20 _____

- _____
- _____
- _____

20 _____

- _____
- _____
- _____

SOME ALL-TIME FAVORITE
TV SHOWS

20 _____

- _____
- _____
- _____

20 _____

- _____
- _____
- _____

20 _____

- _____
- _____
- _____

MY BRAVEST MOMENTS

20 _____

- _____
- _____
- _____

20 _____

- _____
- _____
- _____

20 _____

- _____
- _____
- _____

MEMORABLE OBJECTS OR TOYS FROM CHILDHOOD

20 _____

- _____
- _____
- _____

20 _____

- _____
- _____
- _____

20 _____

- _____
- _____
- _____

JUNE 12

SOME REGRETS

20 _____

- _____
- _____
- _____

20 _____

- _____
- _____
- _____

20 _____

- _____
- _____
- _____

I WOULD LOVE TO...

20 _____

- _____
- _____
- _____

20 _____

- _____
- _____
- _____

20 _____

- _____
- _____
- _____

WISDOM I'D GIVE TO
MY SENIOR CITIZEN SELF

20 _____

- _____
- _____
- _____

20 _____

- _____
- _____
- _____

20 _____

- _____
- _____
- _____

SOME NEW VOCABULARY
WORDS I'VE LEARNED

20 ____

- _____
- _____
- _____

20 ____

- _____
- _____
- _____

20 ____

- _____
- _____
- _____

JOBS I COULD NEVER DO

20 _____

- _____
- _____
- _____

20 _____

- _____
- _____
- _____

20 _____

- _____
- _____
- _____

I THANK MY PARENT(S) FOR...

20 ____

- _____
- _____
- _____

20 ____

- _____
- _____
- _____

20 ____

- _____
- _____
- _____

LITTLE THINGS I APPRECIATE

20 _____

- ------------------------
- ------------------------
- ------------------------

20 _____

- ------------------------
- ------------------------
- ------------------------

20 _____

- ------------------------
- ------------------------
- ------------------------

SOME THINGS I SHOULD BE DOING FOR THE ENVIRONMENT

20 ___

- _____
- _____
- _____

20 ___

- _____
- _____
- _____

20 ___

- _____
- _____
- _____

FAVORITE ARTISTS

20 _____

- _____
- _____
- _____

20 _____

- _____
- _____
- _____

20 _____

- _____
- _____
- _____

AREAS OF MY LIFE THAT NEED IMPROVEMENT

20 _____

- _____
- _____
- _____

20 _____

- _____
- _____
- _____

20 _____

- _____
- _____
- _____

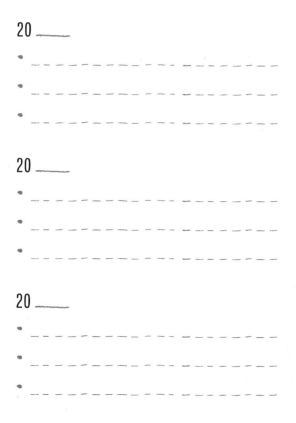

JUNE 22

I BELIEVE...

20 _____

- _____
- _____
- _____

20 _____

- _____
- _____
- _____

20 _____

- _____
- _____
- _____

A FEW RANDOM MEMORIES

20 _____

- _____
- _____
- _____

20 _____

- _____
- _____
- _____

20 _____

- _____
- _____
- _____

GUILTY PLEASURES
RIGHT NOW

20 _____

- _____
- _____
- _____

20 _____

- _____
- _____
- _____

20 _____

- _____
- _____
- _____

THINGS I USED TO DO

20 ____

- _____
- _____
- _____

20 ____

- _____
- _____
- _____

20 ____

- _____
- _____
- _____

CITIES AND COUNTRIES
I WANT TO VISIT

20 _____

- _____
- _____
- _____

20 _____

- _____
- _____
- _____

20 _____

- _____
- _____
- _____

WHAT I HOPE TO
ACCOMPLISH IN FIVE YEARS

20 ____

- _____
- _____
- _____

20 ____

- _____
- _____
- _____

20 ____

- _____
- _____
- _____

RECENT INSPIRATIONS

20 _____

- _____
- _____
- _____

20 _____

- _____
- _____
- _____

20 _____

- _____
- _____
- _____

ADVICE I SHOULD
HAVE LISTENED TO

20 ____

- _____

- _____

- _____

20 ____

- _____

- _____

- _____

20 ____

- _____

- _____

- _____

THINGS THAT MADE ME
HAPPY THIS MONTH

20 _____

- _____
- _____
- _____

20 _____

- _____
- _____
- _____

20 _____

- _____
- _____
- _____

CREATE YOUR OWN LIST

20 _____

- _____

- _____

- _____

20 _____

- _____

- _____

- _____

20 _____

- _____

- _____

- _____

THIS MONTH'S LITTLE
TO-DO LIST

20 ____

- _____
- _____
- _____

20 ____

- _____
- _____
- _____

20 ____

- _____
- _____
- _____

CHARACTER TRAITS I'D DESCRIBE MYSELF AS POSSESSING

20 ___

- _____
- _____
- _____

20 ___

- _____
- _____
- _____

20 ___

- _____
- _____
- _____

THINGS I TAKE FOR
GRANTED SOMETIMES

20 _____

- _____
- _____
- _____

20 _____

- _____
- _____
- _____

20 _____

- _____
- _____
- _____

HARD-TO-REACH PLACES
I WOULD LOVE TO EXPLORE

20 _____

- _____
- _____
- _____

20 _____

- _____
- _____
- _____

20 _____

- _____
- _____
- _____

WORDS TO DESCRIBE
MYSELF TODAY

20 _____

- _____
- _____
- _____

20 _____

- _____
- _____
- _____

20 _____

- _____
- _____
- _____

THREE MEMORIES
I'LL CHERISH FOREVER

20 _____

- _____
- _____
- _____

20 _____

- _____
- _____
- _____

20 _____

- _____
- _____
- _____

TALENTS MY FRIENDS
POSSESS

20 ____

- _____
- _____
- _____

20 ____

- _____
- _____
- _____

20 ____

- _____
- _____
- _____

JULY 8

THANK YOU _____
FOR _____

20 ____

- ---------------------------------
- ---------------------------------
- ---------------------------------

20 ____

- ---------------------------------
- ---------------------------------
- ---------------------------------

20 ____

- ---------------------------------
- ---------------------------------
- ---------------------------------

DESIRABLE QUALITIES
IN A LIFE PARTNER

20 _____

- _____
- _____
- _____

20 _____

- _____
- _____
- _____

20 _____

- _____
- _____
- _____

CHANGES I WISH I COULD MAKE FOR THE WORLD RIGHT NOW

20 _____

- _____
- _____
- _____

20 _____

- _____
- _____
- _____

20 _____

- _____
- _____
- _____

WHAT I NEED
MORE TIME FOR

20 _____

- _____
- _____
- _____

20 _____

- _____
- _____
- _____

20 _____

- _____
- _____
- _____

SOME QUICK CONFESSIONS

20 _____

- _____
- _____
- _____

20 _____

- _____
- _____
- _____

20 _____

- _____
- _____
- _____

CURRENT
FAVORITE TV SHOWS

20 _____

- _____
- _____
- _____

20 _____

- _____
- _____
- _____

20 _____

- _____
- _____
- _____

MEMORABLE MOMENTS
THIS YEAR, SO FAR...

20 ____

- _____
- _____
- _____

20 ____

- _____
- _____
- _____

20 ____

- _____
- _____
- _____

RECENT SPLURGES

20 _____

- _____
- _____
- _____

20 _____

- _____
- _____
- _____

20 _____

- _____
- _____
- _____

THINGS ABOUT MY FAMILY
THAT I'M PROUD OF

20 _____

- ------------------------------
- ------------------------------
- ------------------------------

20 _____

- ------------------------------
- ------------------------------
- ------------------------------

20 _____

- ------------------------------
- ------------------------------
- ------------------------------

FICTIONAL PLACES
I WISH WERE REAL

20 _____

• _____

• _____

• _____

20 _____

• _____

• _____

• _____

20 _____

• _____

• _____

• _____

MY LEAST FAVORITE PEOPLE

20 ____

- _____
- _____
- _____

20 ____

- _____
- _____
- _____

20 ____

- _____
- _____
- _____

CURRENT FAVORITE MEALS

20 ___

- _____
- _____
- _____

20 ___

- _____
- _____
- _____

20 ___

- _____
- _____
- _____

SOME THINGS I DID
THIS WEEK

20 _____

- _____
- _____
- _____

20 _____

- _____
- _____
- _____

20 _____

- _____
- _____
- _____

PEOPLE I MISS

20 _____

- _____
- _____
- _____

20 _____

- _____
- _____
- _____

20 _____

- _____
- _____
- _____

I LOVE TO...

20 _____

- -

- -

- -

20 _____

- -

- -

- -

20 _____

- -

- -

- -

THE LAST TIMES I WAS
OUT IN NATURE

20 ____

- _____
- _____
- _____

20 ____

- _____
- _____
- _____

20 ____

- _____
- _____
- _____

ANIMALS I LOVE

20 ____

- _____
- _____
- _____

20 ____

- _____
- _____
- _____

20 ____

- _____
- _____
- _____

SOME FAVORITE COUPLES

20 _____

- _____
- _____
- _____

20 _____

- _____
- _____
- _____

20 _____

- _____
- _____
- _____

LAST TIMES I'VE DANCED

20 _____

- _____
- _____
- _____

20 _____

- _____
- _____
- _____

20 _____

- _____
- _____
- _____

MY FAVORITE REBELS

20 ___

- _____
- _____
- _____

20 ___

- _____
- _____
- _____

20 ___

- _____
- _____
- _____

MY ANYTHING-GOES DREAM DATE WOULD INCLUDE...

20 _____

- _____
- _____
- _____

20 _____

- _____
- _____
- _____

20 _____

- _____
- _____
- _____

LAST THREE
MOVIES WATCHED

20 _____

- _____
- _____
- _____

20 _____

- _____
- _____
- _____

20 _____

- _____
- _____
- _____

SOME AFFIRMATIONS I NEED TO SAY IN THE MIRROR TODAY

20 ___

- _____
- _____
- _____

20 ___

- _____
- _____
- _____

20 ___

- _____
- _____
- _____

THINGS THAT MADE ME
HAPPY THIS MONTH

20 _____

- _____
- _____
- _____

20 _____

- _____
- _____
- _____

20 _____

- _____
- _____
- _____

THIS MONTH'S LITTLE
TO-DO LIST

20 _____

- _____
- _____
- _____

20 _____

- _____
- _____
- _____

20 _____

- _____
- _____
- _____

I ADMIRE...

20 ___

- _____
- _____
- _____

20 ___

- _____
- _____
- _____

20 ___

- _____
- _____
- _____

SONGS THAT GET
MY BODY GROOVING

20 ___

- _____
- _____
- _____

20 ___

- _____
- _____
- _____

20 ___

- _____
- _____
- _____

NATIONAL PARKS
I'D LIKE TO VISIT

20 _____

- _____
- _____
- _____

20 _____

- _____
- _____
- _____

20 _____

- _____
- _____
- _____

FAVORITE SLANG OR CURSE WORDS

20 ____

- _____
- _____
- _____

20 ____

- _____
- _____
- _____

20 ____

- _____
- _____
- _____

I'D LOVE TO BE
DESCRIBED AS...

20 _____

- _____
- _____
- _____

20 _____

- _____
- _____
- _____

20 _____

- _____
- _____
- _____

WHAT I'D PUT ON MY PROTEST SIGN TODAY

20 _____

- _____
- _____
- _____

20 _____

- _____
- _____
- _____

20 _____

- _____
- _____
- _____

THINGS I'VE
COOKED LATELY

20 ___

- _____
- _____
- _____

20 ___

- _____
- _____
- _____

20 ___

- _____
- _____
- _____

OBJECTS WITH SPECIAL SIGNIFICANCE IN MY HOME

20 _____

- _____
- _____
- _____

20 _____

- _____
- _____
- _____

20 _____

- _____
- _____
- _____

MOST MEMORABLE JOBS

20 ___

- _____
- _____
- _____

20 ___

- _____
- _____
- _____

20 ___

- _____
- _____
- _____

RANDOM THOUGHTS TODAY

20 _____

- _____
- _____
- _____

20 _____

- _____
- _____
- _____

20 _____

- _____
- _____
- _____

MUSEUMS I'D LIKE TO VISIT

20 _____

- _____
- _____
- _____

20 _____

- _____
- _____
- _____

20 _____

- _____
- _____
- _____

I DISLIKE...

20 _____

- _____
- _____
- _____

20 _____

- _____
- _____
- _____

20 _____

- _____
- _____
- _____

THINGS I LOVE ABOUT
THE '70S ERA

20 _____

- _____
- _____
- _____

20 _____

- _____
- _____
- _____

20 _____

- _____
- _____
- _____

GOOD KARMA I'VE
EARNED LATELY

20 _____

- _____
- _____
- _____

20 _____

- _____
- _____
- _____

20 _____

- _____
- _____
- _____

STUFF I'VE GOOGLED RECENTLY

20 _____

- _____
- _____
- _____

20 _____

- _____
- _____
- _____

20 _____

- _____
- _____
- _____

THINGS PEOPLE MIGHT
NOT KNOW ABOUT ME

20 _____

- _____
- _____
- _____

20 _____

- _____
- _____
- _____

20 _____

- _____
- _____
- _____

I LOVE...

20 _____

- _____
- _____
- _____

20 _____

- _____
- _____
- _____

20 _____

- _____
- _____
- _____

WISHES I'D MAKE
RIGHT NOW

20 ____

- _____
- _____
- _____

20 ____

- _____
- _____
- _____

20 ____

- _____
- _____
- _____

FAVORITE NAMES

20 _____

- _____
- _____
- _____

20 _____

- _____
- _____
- _____

20 _____

- _____
- _____
- _____

SMELLS I DISLIKE

20 ____

- _____
- _____
- _____

20 ____

- _____
- _____
- _____

20 ____

- _____
- _____
- _____

TIMES I'VE BEEN
THE MOST SHOCKED

20 _____

- _____
- _____
- _____

20 _____

- _____
- _____
- _____

20 _____

- _____
- _____
- _____

SONGS THAT DESCRIBE MY MOOD THIS WEEK

20 ___

- _____
- _____
- _____

20 ___

- _____
- _____
- _____

20 ___

- _____
- _____
- _____

FRIENDS I HOPE
I KNOW FOREVER

20 ____

- _____
- _____
- _____

20 ____

- _____
- _____
- _____

20 ____

- _____
- _____
- _____

MEMORABLE RESTAURANTS

20 ____

- _____
- _____
- _____

20 ____

- _____
- _____
- _____

20 ____

- _____
- _____
- _____

ANIMALS I'VE SEEN
IN THE WILD

20 _____

- _____

- _____

- _____

20 _____

- _____

- _____

- _____

20 _____

- _____

- _____

- _____

CURRENT COMPLAINTS

20 _____

- _____
- _____
- _____

20 _____

- _____
- _____
- _____

20 _____

- _____
- _____
- _____

CURRENT FAVORITE SONGS

20 _____

- _____
- _____
- _____

20 _____

- _____
- _____
- _____

20 _____

- _____
- _____
- _____

MEMORABLE GIFTS
I'VE RECEIVED

20 ___

- _____
- _____
- _____

20 ___

- _____
- _____
- _____

20 ___

- _____
- _____
- _____

THINGS I LOVE
IN THIS ROOM

20 _____

- _____
- _____
- _____

20 _____

- _____
- _____
- _____

20 _____

- _____
- _____
- _____

THINGS THAT MADE ME
HAPPY THIS MONTH

20 _____

- _____
- _____
- _____

20 _____

- _____
- _____
- _____

20 _____

- _____
- _____
- _____

THIS MONTH'S LITTLE
TO-DO LIST

20 _____

- _____
- _____
- _____

20 _____

- _____
- _____
- _____

20 _____

- _____
- _____
- _____

CURRENT POLITICAL
CONCERNS

20 _____

- _____
- _____
- _____

20 _____

- _____
- _____
- _____

20 _____

- _____
- _____
- _____

BANDS I WISH I COULD HAVE SEEN LIVE

20 _____

- _____
- _____
- _____

20 _____

- _____
- _____
- _____

20 _____

- _____
- _____
- _____

BEST ADVENTURES
FROM THIS SUMMER

20 _____

- _____
- _____
- _____

20 _____

- _____
- _____
- _____

20 _____

- _____
- _____
- _____

IDEAS FOR FUTURE
BIRTHDAYS

20 ____

- _____
- _____
- _____

20 ____

- _____
- _____
- _____

20 ____

- _____
- _____
- _____

RANDOM HIGH SCHOOL MEMORIES

20 ____

- _____
- _____
- _____

20 ____

- _____
- _____
- _____

20 ____

- _____
- _____
- _____

CURRENT DAYDREAMS

20 _____

- _____
- _____
- _____

20 _____

- _____
- _____
- _____

20 _____

- _____
- _____
- _____

BEST THINGS
I'VE EVER EATEN

20 _____

- _____
- _____
- _____

20 _____

- _____
- _____
- _____

20 _____

- _____
- _____
- _____

WORDS TO DESCRIBE TODAY

20 _____

- _____
- _____
- _____

20 _____

- _____
- _____
- _____

20 _____

- _____
- _____
- _____

FAVORITE CLASSES
I'VE TAKEN

20 _____

- _____
- _____
- _____

20 _____

- _____
- _____
- _____

20 _____

- _____
- _____
- _____

MOMENTS I WISH I COULD LIVE AGAIN

20 _____

- _____
- _____
- _____

20 _____

- _____
- _____
- _____

20 _____

- _____
- _____
- _____

THINGS I'M BEING
LAZY ABOUT

20 _____

- _____
- _____
- _____

20 _____

- _____
- _____
- _____

20 _____

- _____
- _____
- _____

MEMORABLE KIDS
FROM CHILDHOOD

20 _____

- _____
- _____
- _____

20 _____

- _____
- _____
- _____

20 _____

- _____
- _____
- _____

I WOULD LOVE TO BE
REINCARNATED INTO...

20 _____

- _____
- _____
- _____

20 _____

- _____
- _____
- _____

20 _____

- _____
- _____
- _____

I HAVE NO INTEREST IN...

20 _____

- _____
- _____
- _____

20 _____

- _____
- _____
- _____

20 _____

- _____
- _____
- _____

NICE THINGS I'D SAY
ABOUT MYSELF TODAY

20 ____

- _____
- _____
- _____

20 ____

- _____
- _____
- _____

20 ____

- _____
- _____
- _____

INTERESTING NEWS STORIES
RIGHT NOW

20 ____

- _____
- _____
- _____

20 ____

- _____
- _____
- _____

20 ____

- _____
- _____
- _____

FAVORS DONE FOR ME
OR I'VE DONE FOR OTHERS

20 _____

- _____
- _____
- _____

20 _____

- _____
- _____
- _____

20 _____

- _____
- _____
- _____

IF I LOST THE ABILITY TO SMELL, I'D MISS SMELLING...

20 ____

- _____
- _____
- _____

20 ____

- _____
- _____
- _____

20 ____

- _____
- _____
- _____

WHAT I ALWAYS NEED
TO REMIND MYSELF

20 _____

- _____
- _____
- _____

20 _____

- _____
- _____
- _____

20 _____

- _____
- _____
- _____

BOOK TITLES FOR MY
LIFE RIGHT NOW

20 _____

- _____
- _____
- _____

20 _____

- _____
- _____
- _____

20 _____

- _____
- _____
- _____

PEOPLE I'M MOST GRATEFUL FOR AT THE MOMENT

20 _____

- _____
- _____
- _____

20 _____

- _____
- _____
- _____

20 _____

- _____
- _____
- _____

WHAT I'D LOVE TO WEAR
TO A COSTUME PARTY

20 _____

- _____
- _____
- _____

20 _____

- _____
- _____
- _____

20 _____

- _____
- _____
- _____

IF I COULD BE SOMEONE ELSE FOR A DAY, I WOULD BE ...

20 ___

- ___
- ___
- ___

20 ___

- ___
- ___
- ___

20 ___

- ___
- ___
- ___

IF I WERE TO GET TATTOOS,
I WOULD GET...

20 ___

- _____
- _____
- _____

20 ___

- _____
- _____
- _____

20 ___

- _____
- _____
- _____

VALUABLE LESSONS
I'VE LEARNED

20 _____

- _____
- _____
- _____

20 _____

- _____
- _____
- _____

20 _____

- _____
- _____
- _____

THINGS I DO THAT WOULD BE SOMEONE ELSE'S PET PEEVE

20 _____

-
-
-

20 _____

-
-
-

20 _____

-
-
-

RECENT CHOICES I'VE MADE

20 _____

- _____
- _____
- _____

20 _____

- _____
- _____
- _____

20 _____

- _____
- _____
- _____

SILLY TOURIST ATTRACTIONS I'VE BEEN TO

20 ____

- _____
- _____
- _____

20 ____

- _____
- _____
- _____

20 ____

- _____
- _____
- _____

THINGS THAT MADE ME HAPPY THIS MONTH

20 _____

- _____
- _____
- _____

20 _____

- _____
- _____
- _____

20 _____

- _____
- _____
- _____

CREATE YOUR OWN LIST

20 _____

- _____
- _____
- _____

20 _____

- _____
- _____
- _____

20 _____

- _____
- _____
- _____

THIS MONTH'S LITTLE TO-DO LIST

20 _____

- _____
- _____
- _____

20 _____

- _____
- _____
- _____

20 _____

- _____
- _____
- _____

FAVORITE WORDS

20 _____

- _____
- _____
- _____

20 _____

- _____
- _____
- _____

20 _____

- _____
- _____
- _____

FICTIONAL FAMILIES
I'D LOVE TO JOIN

20 _____

- _____
- _____
- _____

20 _____

- _____
- _____
- _____

20 _____

- _____
- _____
- _____

RECENT DISAPPOINTMENTS

20 _____

- _____
- _____
- _____

20 _____

- _____
- _____
- _____

20 _____

- _____
- _____
- _____

SONGS WITH
SPECIAL MEANING

20 _____

- _____
- _____
- _____

20 _____

- _____
- _____
- _____

20 _____

- _____
- _____
- _____

THINGS I'D LIKE TO TRY

20 ____

- -
- -
- -

20 ____

- -
- -
- -

20 ____

- -
- -
- -

WHAT I WISH I HAD KNOWN

20 _____

- ------------------------------
- ------------------------------
- ------------------------------

20 _____

- ------------------------------
- ------------------------------
- ------------------------------

20 _____

- ------------------------------
- ------------------------------
- ------------------------------

FILMS OR BOOKS THAT MADE ME CRY

20 ___

- _____
- _____
- _____

20 ___

- _____
- _____
- _____

20 ___

- _____
- _____
- _____

FAVORITE FLAVORS
RIGHT NOW

20 _____

- _____
- _____
- _____

20 _____

- _____
- _____
- _____

20 _____

- _____
- _____
- _____

OCTOBER 10

INSPIRING PEOPLE

20 _____
- _____
- _____
- _____

20 _____
- _____
- _____
- _____

20 _____
- _____
- _____
- _____

SYMBOLS THAT SHOULD BE ON MY FAMILY CREST

20 _____

- _____
- _____
- _____

20 _____

- _____
- _____
- _____

20 _____

- _____
- _____
- _____

WHAT I AM MOST
NOSTALGIC FOR

20 _____

- _____
- _____
- _____

20 _____

- _____
- _____
- _____

20 _____

- _____
- _____
- _____

UNSOLVED MYSTERIES
FROM MY LIFE

20 _____

- _____
- _____
- _____

20 _____

- _____
- _____
- _____

20 _____

- _____
- _____
- _____

WHERE I'D LIKE TO SEE MYSELF IN 25 YEARS

20 _____

- _____
- _____
- _____

20 _____

- _____
- _____
- _____

20 _____

- _____
- _____
- _____

OCTOBER 15

WHAT I LOVE ABOUT:

_____

20 ____

- _____
- _____
- _____

20 ____

- _____
- _____
- _____

20 ____

- _____
- _____
- _____

A FEW RANDOM MEMORIES

20 _____

- _____
- _____
- _____

20 _____

- _____
- _____
- _____

20 _____

- _____
- _____
- _____

RECENT DREAMS
OR NIGHTMARES

20 _____

• _____
• _____
• _____

20 _____

• _____
• _____
• _____

20 _____

• _____
• _____
• _____

FAVORITE THINGS
TO DO AROUND TOWN...

20 _____

- _____
- _____
- _____

20 _____

- _____
- _____
- _____

20 _____

- _____
- _____
- _____

OCTOBER 19

I'M SORRY FOR...

20 _____

- _____
- _____
- _____

20 _____

- _____
- _____
- _____

20 _____

- _____
- _____
- _____

WHAT I'M MOST OPTIMISTIC ABOUT

20 _____

- _____
- _____
- _____

20 _____

- _____
- _____
- _____

20 _____

- _____
- _____
- _____

WORDS THAT CAPTURE
WHO I AM NOT

20 _____

- _____
- _____
- _____

20 _____

- _____
- _____
- _____

20 _____

- _____
- _____
- _____

IF I COULD GO OUT WITH ANYONE TODAY, IT WOULD BE ...

20 ____

- ----------------------------
- ----------------------------
- ----------------------------

20 ____

- ----------------------------
- ----------------------------
- ----------------------------

20 ____

- ----------------------------
- ----------------------------
- ----------------------------

BIGGEST SCARES IN MY LIFE

20 _____

- _____
- _____
- _____

20 _____

- _____
- _____
- _____

20 _____

- _____
- _____
- _____

THINGS THAT MELT
MY STRESS AWAY

20 ____

- ------------------------------
- ------------------------------
- ------------------------------

20 ____

- ------------------------------
- ------------------------------
- ------------------------------

20 ____

- ------------------------------
- ------------------------------
- ------------------------------

THINGS TO DO
IN RETIREMENT

20 _____

- _____
- _____
- _____

20 _____

- _____
- _____
- _____

20 _____

- _____
- _____
- _____

CURRENT WISH LIST

20 _____

- _____
- _____
- _____

20 _____

- _____
- _____
- _____

20 _____

- _____
- _____
- _____

SONGS I WOULD KARAOKE

20 ____

- _____
- _____
- _____

20 ____

- _____
- _____
- _____

20 ____

- _____
- _____
- _____

SCARIEST MOVIES I'VE SEEN

20 ____

- _____
- _____
- _____

20 ____

- _____
- _____
- _____

20 ____

- _____
- _____
- _____

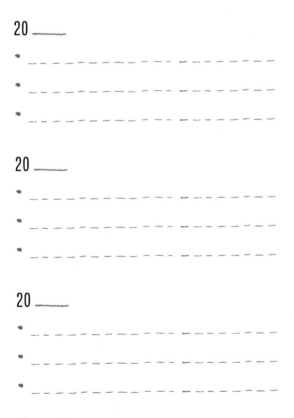

OCTOBER 29

CURRENT FAVORITE
SWEETS

20 _____

- _____
- _____
- _____

20 _____

- _____
- _____
- _____

20 _____

- _____
- _____
- _____

QUESTIONS FOR
THE UNIVERSE

20 ____

- _____
- _____
- _____

20 ____

- _____
- _____
- _____

20 ____

- _____
- _____
- _____

THINGS THAT MADE ME
HAPPY THIS MONTH

20 _____

- _____
- _____
- _____

20 _____

- _____
- _____
- _____

20 _____

- _____
- _____
- _____

THIS MONTH'S LITTLE
TO-DO LIST

20 _____

- _____
- _____
- _____

20 _____

- _____
- _____
- _____

20 _____

- _____
- _____
- _____

BIGGEST CRIES
OF MY LIFETIME

20 _____

- _____
- _____
- _____

20 _____

- _____
- _____
- _____

20 _____

- _____
- _____
- _____

NOVEMBER 3

REMINDERS FOR
WHEN I'M DOWN

20 _____

- _____
- _____
- _____

20 _____

- _____
- _____
- _____

20 _____

- _____
- _____
- _____

THINGS I LOVE ABOUT
THE '60S ERA

20 _____

- _____
- _____
- _____

20 _____

- _____
- _____
- _____

20 _____

- _____
- _____
- _____

MOMENTS IN HISTORY I WISH I COULD HAVE BEEN THERE FOR

20 ____

- _____
- _____
- _____

20 ____

- _____
- _____
- _____

20 ____

- _____
- _____
- _____

SOME STUFF THAT ISN'T GREAT RIGHT NOW

20 _____

- _____
- _____
- _____

20 _____

- _____
- _____
- _____

20 _____

- _____
- _____
- _____

WHAT GIVES ME HOPE

20 ___

- _____
- _____
- _____

20 ___

- _____
- _____
- _____

20 ___

- _____
- _____
- _____

FICTIONAL CHARACTERS I'M LIKE OR ASPIRE TO BE LIKE

20 _____

- _____
- _____
- _____

20 _____

- _____
- _____
- _____

20 _____

- _____
- _____
- _____

NOVEMBER 9

I WISH THERE
WAS AN APP FOR...

20 ___

- _____
- _____
- _____

20 ___

- _____
- _____
- _____

20 ___

- _____
- _____
- _____

MY BEST QUALITIES

20 _____

- _____
- _____
- _____

20 _____

- _____
- _____
- _____

20 _____

- _____
- _____
- _____

MARRIAGE/UNION CEREMONY VOWS MOST IMPORTANT TO ME

20 ____

- _____
- _____
- _____

20 ____

- _____
- _____
- _____

20 ____

- _____
- _____
- _____

TRAVEL WISH LIST

20 _____

- _____
- _____
- _____

20 _____

- _____
- _____
- _____

20 _____

- _____
- _____
- _____

MEMORABLE THINGS THAT WERE IN MY CHILDHOOD HOME

20 _____

- _____
- _____
- _____

20 _____

- _____
- _____
- _____

20 _____

- _____
- _____
- _____

NOVEMBER 14

SOME THINGS
I DID THIS WEEK

20 _____

- _____
- _____
- _____

20 _____

- _____
- _____
- _____

20 _____

- _____
- _____
- _____

NICKNAMES I'VE HAD
OR COULD HAVE HAD

20 ___

- _____
- _____
- _____

20 ___

- _____
- _____
- _____

20 ___

- _____
- _____
- _____

GAME SHOWS
OR GAMES I LOVE

20 ____

- _____
- _____
- _____

20 ____

- _____
- _____
- _____

20 ____

- _____
- _____
- _____

I WOULD NEVER...

20 _____

- _____
- _____
- _____

20 _____

- _____
- _____
- _____

20 _____

- _____
- _____
- _____

LAST THREE
MOVIES WATCHED

20 ___

- _____
- _____
- _____

20 ___

- _____
- _____
- _____

20 ___

- _____
- _____
- _____

NOVEMBER 19

WHAT I DISLIKE ABOUT:

_____

20 _____

- _____
- _____
- _____

20 _____

- _____
- _____
- _____

20 _____

- _____
- _____
- _____

RANDOM THOUGHTS TODAY

20 _____

- _____
- _____
- _____

20 _____

- _____
- _____
- _____

20 _____

- _____
- _____
- _____

FAVORITE THINGS
TO DO LATELY

20 _____

- _____
- _____
- _____

20 _____

- _____
- _____
- _____

20 _____

- _____
- _____
- _____

NOVEMBER 22

THINGS I'M MOST GRATEFUL
FOR AT THE MOMENT

20 _____

- _____
- _____
- _____

20 _____

- _____
- _____
- _____

20 _____

- _____
- _____
- _____

WORDS TO DESCRIBE
MYSELF TODAY

20 _____

- _____
- _____
- _____

20 _____

- _____
- _____
- _____

20 _____

- _____
- _____
- _____

CURRENT FEMALE CRUSHES

20 ____

- _____
- _____
- _____

20 ____

- _____
- _____
- _____

20 ____

- _____
- _____
- _____

THINGS THAT
MELT MY HEART

20 _____

- _____
- _____
- _____

20 _____

- _____
- _____
- _____

20 _____

- _____
- _____
- _____

WHAT I'D HAVE
AT MY LAST MEAL

20 _____

• _____

• _____

• _____

20 _____

• _____

• _____

• _____

20 _____

• _____

• _____

• _____

MEMORABLE DINNERS
OR PARTIES

20 _____

- _____
- _____
- _____

20 _____

- _____
- _____
- _____

20 _____

- _____
- _____
- _____

BIGGEST SPLURGES
IN MY LIFE

20 _____

- _____
- _____
- _____

20 _____

- _____
- _____
- _____

20 _____

- _____
- _____
- _____

JOBS PEOPLE IN MY FAMILY TREE HAVE HAD

20 _____

- _____
- _____
- _____

20 _____

- _____
- _____
- _____

20 _____

- _____
- _____
- _____

THINGS THAT MADE ME
HAPPY THIS MONTH

20 ___

- _____
- _____
- _____

20 ___

- _____
- _____
- _____

20 ___

- _____
- _____
- _____

CREATE YOUR OWN LIST

20 _____

- _____
- _____
- _____

20 _____

- _____
- _____
- _____

20 _____

- _____
- _____
- _____

THIS MONTH'S LITTLE
TO-DO LIST

20 _____

- _____

- _____

- _____

20 _____

- _____

- _____

- _____

20 _____

- _____

- _____

- _____

A FEW MANTRAS
FOR ME RIGHT NOW

20 ____

- _____
- _____
- _____

20 ____

- _____
- _____
- _____

20 ____

- _____
- _____
- _____

THINGS I SEE IN MY
DAY-TO-DAY THAT I LOVE ...

20 _____

- _____
- _____
- _____

20 _____

- _____
- _____
- _____

20 _____

- _____
- _____
- _____

BEST TV SHOWS THIS YEAR

20 _____

- _____
- _____
- _____

20 _____

- _____
- _____
- _____

20 _____

- _____
- _____
- _____

MOST MEMORABLE SMELLS

20 _____

- _____
- _____
- _____

20 _____

- _____
- _____
- _____

20 _____

- _____
- _____
- _____

ACCOMPLISHMENTS
FROM THIS PAST YEAR

20 _____

- _____
- _____
- _____

20 _____

- _____
- _____
- _____

20 _____

- _____
- _____
- _____

NEW PEOPLE
I'VE MET THIS YEAR

20 _____

- _____
- _____
- _____

20 _____

- _____
- _____
- _____

20 _____

- _____
- _____
- _____

MEMORABLE PLACES
I WENT THIS YEAR

20 ____

- _____
- _____
- _____

20 ____

- _____
- _____
- _____

20 ____

- _____
- _____
- _____

CONCERTS I WENT
TO THIS YEAR

20 ____

- _____
- _____
- _____

20 ____

- _____
- _____
- _____

20 ____

- _____
- _____
- _____

MY IDEA OF
HEAVEN WOULD BE ...

20 ____

- _____
- _____
- _____

20 ____

- _____
- _____
- _____

20 ____

- _____
- _____
- _____

MOMENTS THAT WOULD BE IN MY AUTOBIOGRAPHY

20 _____

- _____
- _____
- _____

20 _____

- _____
- _____
- _____

20 _____

- _____
- _____
- _____

SOME NICE THINGS PEOPLE HAVE DONE FOR ME

20 ____

- _____
- _____
- _____

20 ____

- _____
- _____
- _____

20 ____

- _____
- _____
- _____

I WILL NEVER
UNDERSTAND WHY...

20 _____

- _____
- _____
- _____

20 _____

- _____
- _____
- _____

20 _____

- _____
- _____
- _____

NEW RESTAURANTS
I TRIED THIS YEAR

20 ____

- _____
- _____
- _____

20 ____

- _____
- _____
- _____

20 ____

- _____
- _____
- _____

THINGS TO
LOOK FORWARD TO

20 _____

- _____
- _____
- _____

20 _____

- _____
- _____
- _____

20 _____

- _____
- _____
- _____

A FEW THINGS
I'D CHANGE RIGHT NOW

20 _____

- _____
- _____
- _____

20 _____

- _____
- _____
- _____

20 _____

- _____
- _____
- _____

IF I WERE A BIRD, I'D FLY TO THE FOLLOWING PLACES TODAY

20 _____

- _____
- _____
- _____

20 _____

- _____
- _____
- _____

20 _____

- _____
- _____
- _____

HARDEST MOMENTS
FROM THIS YEAR

20 _____

- _____
- _____
- _____

20 _____

- _____
- _____
- _____

20 _____

- _____
- _____
- _____

FAVORITE GET-TOGETHERS
FROM THIS YEAR

20 ____

- _____
- _____
- _____

20 ____

- _____
- _____
- _____

20 ____

- _____
- _____
- _____

I WON'T TRY THIS AGAIN

20 _____

- _____
- _____
- _____

20 _____

- _____
- _____
- _____

20 _____

- _____
- _____
- _____

SONGS THAT
CAPTURE THIS YEAR

20 _____

- _____
- _____
- _____

20 _____

- _____
- _____
- _____

20 _____

- _____
- _____
- _____

FAVORITE FILMS
FROM THIS YEAR

20 ___

- _____
- _____
- _____

20 ___

- _____
- _____
- _____

20 ___

- _____
- _____
- _____

FAVORITE READS THIS YEAR

20 _____

- --
- --
- --

20 _____

- --
- --
- --

20 _____

- --
- --
- --

DONATIONS OR GIFTS
I GAVE THIS YEAR

20 _____

- _____
- _____
- _____

20 _____

- _____
- _____
- _____

20 _____

- _____
- _____
- _____

HIGHLIGHTS FROM
THIS PAST YEAR

20 _____

- _____
- _____
- _____

20 _____

- _____
- _____
- _____

20 _____

- _____
- _____
- _____

FAVORITE SOUNDS

20 _____

- _____
- _____
- _____

20 _____

- _____
- _____
- _____

20 _____

- _____
- _____
- _____

MEMORABLE STORIES
IN THE NEWS THIS YEAR

20 ___

- _____
- _____
- _____

20 ___

- _____
- _____
- _____

20 ___

- _____
- _____
- _____

THE UNEXPECTED THAT
HAPPENED THIS YEAR

20 _____

- _____
- _____
- _____

20 _____

- _____
- _____
- _____

20 _____

- _____
- _____
- _____

PREDICTIONS
FOR NEXT YEAR

20 _____

- _____
- _____
- _____

20 _____

- _____
- _____
- _____

20 _____

- _____
- _____
- _____

SOME THINGS TO SAY
IN THE MIRROR TODAY

20 _____

• _____

• _____

• _____

20 _____

• _____

• _____

• _____

20 _____

• _____

• _____

• _____

THINGS THAT MADE ME
HAPPY THIS MONTH

20 _____

- _____

- _____

- _____

20 _____

- _____

- _____

- _____

20 _____

- _____

- _____

- _____

DATES TO REMEMBER

NOTES